Bucket List

Why do you want to create a bucket list? Ha... travelling shows, or maybe even the movie ... and decided that you were not getting any y... know, time has never slowed down, or stopped for you, and this was something you had to do? Maybe you have an itch or inklings of doing things that would be on a bucket list, but never had the chance to do them because life got in the way, or you were too busy chasing that dollar – working your butt off...all so you could keep up with the Joneses? Only you didn't know that the Joneses had their own bucket list and was living their life, not leaving it behind.

For me, one of my bucket list items was something that I had always wanted to do since I graduated high school, and that was to travel across the USA, and visit neat and unique places along the way, which included a lot of National Parks, Monuments, museums, and the Pacific ocean. I had never been west of Tennessee; can you believe that? And it was scary at first, but as I mapped my way from city to city it got easier, and to be honest, once I left North Carolina the sick feeling in my stomach I had from not knowing what was ahead abated. I have always enjoyed photography and imagined myself traveling to lots of great places and getting some amazing photos so that I could look back one day and not ever have the regret that I didn't do it and could have. I could look at a map and say that I was there!! I could look at a photo and tell the younger members of my extended family what I was doing at that moment in time and what it was all about. I did this at age 52...so as you can see, it is never too late to do things that might be on your bucket list. So, ask yourself, why do you want to create a bucket list?

175 Examples that might inspire you to form your bucket list.

1. Arrive at your destination by seaplane.
2. Surf's up - try surfing.
3. Try zip lining.
4. Go caving.
5. Get a tattoo.
6. Swim with dolphins.
7. Try hang gliding.
8. Go on a hot air balloon ride.
9. Try skydiving.
10. Try kite surfing.
11. Try paddle boarding.
12. Try kayaking.
13. Try parasailing.
14. Try playing a game of paint ball.
15. Try driving a nascar.
16. Try rappelling down a cliff or waterfall.
17. Try snow skiing.
18. Try snowboarding.
19. Try Scuba diving.
20. Swim with sharks.
21. Go Whitewater rafting?
22. Walk a suspension bridge.
23. Attend a rodeo.
24. Attend a Nascar race.
25. Attend a formula one race.
26. Climb a tree.
27. Hike to the top of a volcano.
28. Attend a horse race.
29. Chase a tornado.
30. Drive an ATV or motorcycle.
31. Ride a fan boat in the everglades.
32. Travel overseas.
33. Take a vacation on a dude ranch and herd cattle.
34. Hike every trail in your state.
35. Go flounder or frog gigging.
36. Go horseback riding on a beach somewhere.
37. Go whale watching.
38. Try bird watching.
39. Hug a Sequoia tree.
40. Dance in the rain.
41. Build a snowman.
42. Try riding a horse and carriage.
43. See a coral reef.
44. Name a star.

This Bucket List Journal Belongs To –

Ellie & James

Copyright © 2021 by Author – Memphis Doyle

All Rights Reserved.
No part of this book may be used or reproduced by any means, graphic, electronic, or mechanical, including photocopying, recording, taping, or by any information storage retrieval system without the written permission of the publisher except in the case of brief quotations embodied in critical articles and reviews.

Editing By – Memphis Doyle
Back Cover Image By – Memphis Doyle
Book Design and Illustration By – Memphis Doyle
Grand Tetons photo inside book By – Memphis Doyle

First Available 2021
Publisher Name – Jester Media Publishing

Whitewater Rafting

Pacific Crest Trail

Disneyworld

New Zealand

45. Milk a cow.
46. See the salmon run.
47. Stay overnight in a barn and sleep in the hay loft.
48. Dive into a huge pile of leaves.
49. Stand under a waterfall.
50. Swim with sea turtles.
51. Release sea turtles into the ocean.
52. Swim with manatees.
53. Sleep in a yurt.
54. Sleep in an igloo.
55. Sleep in a teepee.
56. Sleep under the stars.
57. Visit a dark skies location and stay overnight to do night photography.
58. Watch some celestial event with binoculars or telescope.
59. Walk on a black sand beach.
60. Attend your high school reunion.
61. Take a class in photography or some other interest like cooking.
62. Host a family reunion.
63. Get married.
64. Go on a blind date.
65. Test your fears by riding the scariest ride at the state fair.
66. Ride a rollercoaster.
67. Help a homeless person.
68. Adopt a dog from the pound.
69. Meet someone famous.
70. Kiss a stranger.
71. Plan a date night with your spouse or significant other.
72. Organize a family portrait.
73. Sing karaoke.
74. Reconnect with an old friend.
75. Share a cab with a stranger.
76. Stay up all night talking with someone.
77. Visit your childhood home.
78. Camp out with your kids under a blanket tent in the living room.
79. Write your significant other a love letter.
80. Get published.
81. Write a book.
82. Blow glass.
83. Try quilting and complete a quilt.
84. Try cross stitching and complete a pattern.
85. Do a family tree search and learn about your past.
86. Create a piece of art and sell it.
87. Create a design for a blank tee shirt.
88. Design a website.

89. Create a blog.
90. Make a calendar with your own photos.
91. Knit or crochet a blanket or beanie.
92. Make a scented candle.
93. Make a handmade gift for someone.
94. Make a tie dye shirt.
95. Create a scrapbook.
96. Learn how to make origami.
97. Create a stained-glass window or piece of artwork.
98. Refinish an old piece of furniture.
99. Build a piece of furniture.
100. Create a photo coffee table book.
101. Go to the opera.
102. Attend an orchestra.
103. Attend a concert of favorite band or singer.
104. Visit a jazz club.
105. Attend the Day of the Dead festival.
106. Visit New Orleans during Mardi Gras
107. Attend an art gallery opening.
108. Attend a masquerade ball.
109. Learn how to ballroom dance.
110. Attend a boxing match.
111. Attend a pro football game.
112. Attend a murder mystery dinner.
113. Visit all the US National Parks.
114. Visit all 50 states.
115. Attend running of the bulls.
116. Make a bet at either the horse or dog races.
117. Create a You-tube video.
118. Attend a march or rally of protest.
119. Have a caricature drawing of yourself done.
120. Go on a cruise.
121. Attend a blues bar.
122. Attend a dinner theater.
123. Visit another country or more many times.
124. Go to a drive-in movie.
125. Attend Comicon.
126. Learn to line dance.
127. Learn to play a musical instrument i.e., Harmonica, guitar etc.
128. Play Bingo at a bingo hall.
129. Volunteer at a soup kitchen, homeless shelter, or nursing home.
130. Visit Ripley's Believe it or not.
131. Visit Disneyworld or Disneyland.
132. Ride a mechanical bull.

133. See a Ballet.
134. Attend a Broadway play.
135. See a Cirque du Soleil Show.
136. Visit the seven wonders of the world.
137. See a 3D movie.
138. Ride a very tall Ferris Wheel.
139. See a Las Vegas show.
140. Do a night of gambling at a casino.
141. Read the top 100 books of all time.
142. Dye your hair in a crazy color.
143. Do a spa treatment for yourself.
144. Visit a physic and have your palm read.
145. Grow a home garden.
146. Try canning to preserve food.
147. Create and build a business.
148. Make a career out of hobby.
149. Attend a beer festival.
150. Attend a lobster fest in New England.
151. Visit a distillery and taste their products.
152. Drink some Absinthe.
153. Try an alcoholic drink that scares you.
154. Try moonshine.
155. Drink Sake.
156. Go wine tasting.
157. Visit an orchard and pick and eat fruit from the tree.
158. Try deep fried anything at the local state fair.
159. Fly in a plane.
160. Build a sandcastle.
161. Visit and stay overnight at a haunted location.
162. Investigate an Urban legend.
163. Learn to play chess.
164. Build a model ca, plane, or ship.
165. Rope swing into water.
166. Go skinny dipping.
167. Smoke a doobie.
168. Be a mentor to someone who needs it.
169. Donate unneeded possessions to charity.
170. Entertain the elderly at a nursing home.
171. Donate books, games, puzzles, and activity books to a nursing home.
172. Foster a displaced or injured animal.
173. Get your college degree (not that it is needed, but if you want to).
174. Pay it forward.
175. Send a care package to a soldier.

Bucket List Index	Completed	☑
	1	☐
	2	☐
	3	☐
	4	☐
	5	☐
	6	☐
	7	☐
	8	☐
	9	☐
	10	☐
	11	☐
	12	☐
	13	☐
	14	☐
	15	☐
	16	☐
	17	☐
	18	☐
	19	☐
	20	☐
	21	☐
	22	☐
	23	☐
	24	☐
	25	☐

Bucket List Index	Completed	☑
	26	☐
	27	☐
	28	☐
	29	☐
	30	☐
	31	☐
	32	☐
	33	☐
	34	☐
	35	☐
	36	☐
	37	☐
	38	☐
	39	☐
	40	☐
	41	☐
	42	☐
	43	☐
	44	☐
	45	☐
	46	☐
	47	☐
	48	☐
	49	☐
	50	☐

Bucket List Index	Completed	✓
	51	☐
	52	☐
	53	☐
	54	☐
	55	☐
	56	☐
	57	☐
	58	☐
	59	☐
	60	☐
	61	☐
	62	☐
	63	☐
	64	☐
	65	☐
	66	☐
	67	☐
	68	☐
	69	☐
	70	☐
	71	☐
	72	☐
	73	☐
	74	☐
	75	☐

Bucket List Index	Completed	☑
	76	☐
	77	☐
	78	☐
	79	☐
	80	☐
	81	☐
	82	☐
	83	☐
	84	☐
	85	☐
	86	☐
	87	☐
	88	☐
	89	☐
	90	☐
	91	☐
	92	☐
	93	☐
	94	☐
	95	☐
	96	☐
	97	☐
	98	☐
	99	☐
	100	☐

Special Thanks!

Thank you so much for purchasing this journal. Please consider leaving a review and checking out our Amazon collection with more "Outdoor Adventure" titles to come. I hope you get lots of use from this journal, and that it serves you well for many bucket list items to come. Enjoy your time in the outdoors and in whatever you do, and I humbly ask that you leave it the way you found it when doing outdoor activities. Pack it in, pack it out!

If you like this book, take a look at other great Notebooks and Journals by clicking on the author link "Memphis Doyle" near the top of page under the title of book. Thanks.

_____

Gift Idea:

If this is a gift for someone, you might want to use the next page to offer a Happy birthday or some other type of greeting, or any memorable experiences you have had with them to give them something to reminisce about while they come up with their own bucket list. They will appreciate it, and probably look upon this page often.

To:_____

Notes:

Notes:

Notes:

Notes:

Notes:

Notes:

Notes:

1

Date: _____

Travel to Anglesey

Why we want to do this. Celebrate 5 years as a couple in a beautiful place. Explore more and have further adventures

Our Plan to make this happen. Book an airbnb
- Book a day off work
- Plan activities
- Take lots of pictures!!

←――――― ⋘ Let's Do This! ⋙ ―――――→

Completion Date _____ **Location** _____

Our Story

Our Favorite Memories

Would We Recommend This To Others? Yes ☐ No ☐
Would We Do It Again? Yes ☐ No ☐

2

Date: _____

_____
_____
_____

Why we want to do this.

_____
_____
_____
_____

Our Plan to make this happen.

_____
_____
_____
_____

⇐⇐⇐ **Let's Do This!** ⇛⇛⇛

Completion Date _____ Location _____

Our Story

_____
_____
_____
_____
_____
_____

Our Favorite Memories

_____
_____
_____

Would We Recommend This To Others?   Yes ☐   No ☐
Would We Do It Again?   Yes ☐   No ☐

3

Date:

Why we want to do this.

Our Plan to make this happen.

⟵ ⋘ Let's Do This! ⋙ ⟶

Completion Date   **Location**

Our Story

Our Favorite Memories

Would We Recommend This To Others?   Yes ☐   No ☐
Would We Do It Again?   Yes ☐   No ☐

4

Date:

Why we want to do this.

Our Plan to make this happen.

<<< Let's Do This! >>>

Completion Date   Location

Our Story

Our Favorite Memories

Would We Recommend This To Others?   Yes ☐   No ☐
Would We Do It Again?   Yes ☐   No ☐

5

Date:

Why we want to do this.

Our Plan to make this happen.

Let's Do This!

Completion Date   **Location**

Our Story

Our Favorite Memories

Would We Recommend This To Others?   Yes ☐   No ☐

Would We Do It Again?   Yes ☐   No ☐

6

Date: _____

Why we want to do this.

Our Plan to make this happen.

<<< **Let's Do This!** >>>

Completion Date _____ Location _____

Our Story

Our Favorite Memories

Would We Recommend This To Others? Yes ☐ No ☐
Would We Do It Again? Yes ☐ No ☐

7

Date: _____

_____
_____

Why we want to do this.

_____
_____
_____

Our Plan to make this happen.

_____
_____
_____

<<< **Let's Do This!** >>>

Completion Date _____ **Location** _____

Our Story

_____
_____
_____
_____

Our Favorite Memories

_____
_____

Would We Recommend This To Others?   Yes ☐   No ☐
Would We Do It Again?   Yes ☐   No ☐

8

Date:

Why we want to do this.

Our Plan to make this happen.

<<< Let's Do This! >>>

Completion Date	Location

Our Story

Our Favorite Memories

Would We Recommend This To Others? Yes ☐ No ☐
Would We Do It Again? Yes ☐ No ☐

9

Date:

Why we want to do this.

Our Plan to make this happen.

⟵―――――⋘ Let's Do This! ⋙―――――⟶

Completion Date　　　　　Location

Our Story

Our Favorite Memories

Would We Recommend This To Others?　Yes ☐　No ☐

Would We Do It Again?　Yes ☐　No ☐

10

Date: _____

_____
_____

Why we want to do this.
_____
_____
_____
_____

Our Plan to make this happen.
_____
_____
_____
_____

⟵————— ⋘ Let's Do This! ⋙ —————⟶

Completion Date _____   Location _____

Our Story
_____
_____
_____
_____
_____
_____

Our Favorite Memories
_____
_____
_____

Would We Recommend This To Others?   Yes ☐   No ☐
Would We Do It Again?   Yes ☐   No ☐

11

Date:

Why we want to do this.

Our Plan to make this happen.

⟵ ⋘ **Let's Do This!** ⋙ ⟶

Completion Date **Location**

Our Story

Our Favorite Memories

Would We Recommend This To Others? Yes ☐ No ☐
Would We Do It Again? Yes ☐ No ☐

12

Date: _____

Why we want to do this.

Our Plan to make this happen.

⟵————⫷⫷⫷ Let's Do This! ⫸⫸⫸————⟶

Completion Date _____   Location _____

Our Story

Our Favorite Memories

Would We Recommend This To Others?   Yes ☐   No ☐
Would We Do It Again?   Yes ☐   No ☐

13

Date:

Why we want to do this.

Our Plan to make this happen.

⟵———————⟪⟪⟪ **Let's Do This!** ⟫⟫⟫———————⟶

Completion Date   **Location**

Our Story

Our Favorite Memories

Would We Recommend This To Others?   Yes ☐   No ☐
Would We Do It Again?   Yes ☐   No ☐

14

Date: _____

_____
_____

Why we want to do this.
_____
_____
_____

Our Plan to make this happen.
_____
_____
_____
_____

⟵——————⋘ **Let's Do This!** ⋙——————⟶

Completion Date _____ **Location** _____

Our Story _____
_____
_____
_____
_____
_____

Our Favorite Memories
_____
_____
_____
_____

Would We Recommend This To Others?   Yes ☐   No ☐
Would We Do It Again?   Yes ☐   No ☐

15

Date: _____

Why we want to do this.

_____
_____
_____

Our Plan to make this happen.

_____
_____
_____

←——————— ⟪ Let's Do This! ⟫ ———————→

Completion Date _____ **Location** _____

Our Story

_____
_____
_____
_____

Our Favorite Memories

_____
_____

Would We Recommend This To Others?   Yes ☐   No ☐
Would We Do It Again?   Yes ☐   No ☐

16

Date: _____

Why we want to do this.

_____
_____
_____
_____

Our Plan to make this happen.

_____
_____
_____

⟵————⟪⟪ Let's Do This! ⟫⟫————⟶

Completion Date _____ Location _____

Our Story

_____
_____
_____
_____
_____

Our Favorite Memories

_____
_____
_____

Would We Recommend This To Others?   Yes ☐   No ☐
Would We Do It Again?   Yes ☐   No ☐

17

Date: _____

_____
_____
_____

Why we want to do this.

_____
_____
_____
_____

Our Plan to make this happen.

_____
_____
_____
_____

⟵————————⟪⟨ **Let's Do This!** ⟩⟫————————⟶

Completion Date _____ **Location** _____

Our Story

_____
_____
_____
_____
_____
_____

Our Favorite Memories

_____
_____
_____

Would We Recommend This To Others?   Yes ☐   No ☐
Would We Do It Again?   Yes ☐   No ☐

18

Date: _____

Why we want to do this.

Our Plan to make this happen.

⟵——— ⋘ **Let's Do This!** ⋙ ———⟶

Completion Date _____ **Location** _____

Our Story

Our Favorite Memories

Would We Recommend This To Others?   Yes ☐   No ☐
Would We Do It Again?   Yes ☐   No ☐

19

Date:

Why we want to do this.

Our Plan to make this happen.

⇐ ⋘ Let's Do This! ⋙ ⇒

Completion Date   Location

Our Story

Our Favorite Memories

Would We Recommend This To Others?   Yes ☐   No ☐
Would We Do It Again?   Yes ☐   No ☐

20

Date: _____

_____

_____

Why we want to do this.

_____
_____
_____
_____

Our Plan to make this happen.

_____
_____
_____
_____

<<< **Let's Do This!** >>>

Completion Date _____   Location _____

Our Story

_____
_____
_____
_____
_____
_____

Our Favorite Memories

_____
_____
_____

Would We Recommend This To Others?   Yes ☐   No ☐
Would We Do It Again?   Yes ☐   No ☐

21

Date: _____

Why we want to do this.

Our Plan to make this happen.

⟵————————⟪⟪⟪ **Let's Do This!** ⟫⟫⟫————————⟶

Completion Date   Location

Our Story

Our Favorite Memories

Would We Recommend This To Others?   Yes ☐   No ☐
Would We Do It Again?   Yes ☐   No ☐

22

Date: _____

_____
_____

Why we want to do this.

_____
_____
_____
_____

Our Plan to make this happen.

_____
_____
_____
_____

⟵————— ⋘ **Let's Do This!** ⋙ —————⟶

Completion Date _____   **Location** _____

Our Story

_____
_____
_____
_____
_____

Our Favorite Memories

_____
_____
_____

Would We Recommend This To Others?   Yes ☐   No ☐
Would We Do It Again?   Yes ☐   No ☐

23

Date: _____

_____

Why we want to do this.

_____
_____
_____
_____

Our Plan to make this happen.

_____
_____
_____
_____

⟵———— ⋘ **Let's Do This!** ⋙ ————⟶

Completion Date _____ **Location** _____

Our Story

_____
_____
_____
_____
_____

Our Favorite Memories

_____
_____
_____

Would We Recommend This To Others?   Yes ☐   No ☐

Would We Do It Again?   Yes ☐   No ☐

24

Date: _____

Why we want to do this.

Our Plan to make this happen.

⟵ ⟪ Let's Do This! ⟫ ⟶

Completion Date _____ Location _____

Our Story

Our Favorite Memories

Would We Recommend This To Others?   Yes ☐   No ☐
Would We Do It Again?   Yes ☐   No ☐

25

Date:

Why we want to do this.

Our Plan to make this happen.

⟵————⟪⟪ Let's Do This! ⟫⟫————⟶

Completion Date **Location**

Our Story

Our Favorite Memories

Would We Recommend This To Others? Yes ☐ No ☐
Would We Do It Again? Yes ☐ No ☐

26

Date:

Why we want to do this.

Our Plan to make this happen.

<<< Let's Do This! >>>

Completion Date   Location

Our Story

Our Favorite Memories

Would We Recommend This To Others?   Yes ☐   No ☐
Would We Do It Again?   Yes ☐   No ☐

27

Date:

Why we want to do this.

Our Plan to make this happen.

⇐———————⋘ **Let's Do This!** ⋙———————⇒

Completion Date **Location**

Our Story

Our Favorite Memories

Would We Recommend This To Others?   Yes ☐   No ☐

Would We Do It Again?   Yes ☐   No ☐

28

Date: _____

Why we want to do this.

Our Plan to make this happen.

⟵——— ⫷⫷⫷ **Let's Do This!** ⫸⫸⫸ ———⟶

Completion Date _____ **Location** _____

Our Story

Our Favorite Memories

Would We Recommend This To Others?   Yes ☐   No ☐
Would We Do It Again?   Yes ☐   No ☐

29

Date:

Why we want to do this.

Our Plan to make this happen.

←——— ⟨⟨⟨ Let's Do This! ⟩⟩⟩ ———→

Completion Date　　　　　Location

Our Story

Our Favorite Memories

Would We Recommend This To Others?　Yes ☐　No ☐
Would We Do It Again?　Yes ☐　No ☐

30

Date: _____

Why we want to do this.

Our Plan to make this happen.

⟵ ⋘ **Let's Do This!** ⋙ ⟶

Completion Date _____ **Location** _____

Our Story

Our Favorite Memories

Would We Recommend This To Others? Yes ☐ No ☐
Would We Do It Again? Yes ☐ No ☐

31

Date:

Why we want to do this.

Our Plan to make this happen.

<<< Let's Do This! >>>

Completion Date   Location

Our Story

Our Favorite Memories

Would We Recommend This To Others?   Yes ☐   No ☐
Would We Do It Again?   Yes ☐   No ☐

32

Date:

Why we want to do this.

Our Plan to make this happen.

⟵————————⟪⟪⟪ Let's Do This! ⟫⟫⟫————————⟶

Completion Date   Location

Our Story

Our Favorite Memories

Would We Recommend This To Others?   Yes ☐   No ☐
Would We Do It Again?   Yes ☐   No ☐

33

Date:

Why we want to do this.

Our Plan to make this happen.

Let's Do This!

Completion Date   Location

Our Story

Our Favorite Memories

Would We Recommend This To Others?   Yes ☐   No ☐
Would We Do It Again?   Yes ☐   No ☐

34

Date: _____

_____
_____
_____

Why we want to do this.

_____
_____
_____

Our Plan to make this happen.

_____
_____
_____

⟵─────────── ⋘ Let's Do This! ⋙ ───────────⟶

Completion Date _____ **Location** _____

Our Story

_____
_____
_____
_____

Our Favorite Memories

_____
_____
_____

Would We Recommend This To Others? Yes ☐   No ☐
Would We Do It Again? Yes ☐   No ☐

35

Date:

Why we want to do this.

Our Plan to make this happen.

<<< Let's Do This! >>>

Completion Date   Location

Our Story

Our Favorite Memories

Would We Recommend This To Others?   Yes ☐   No ☐
Would We Do It Again?   Yes ☐   No ☐

36

Date: _____

_____

_____

Why we want to do this. _____

_____

_____

_____

Our Plan to make this happen.

_____

_____

_____

⟵————————⋘ **Let's Do This!** ⋙————————⟶

Completion Date _____ **Location** _____

Our Story _____

_____

_____

_____

_____

Our Favorite Memories _____

_____

_____

Would We Recommend This To Others?   Yes ☐   No ☐
Would We Do It Again?   Yes ☐   No ☐

37

Date:

Why we want to do this.

Our Plan to make this happen.

⟵⟵⟵ Let's Do This! ⟶⟶⟶

Completion Date   Location

Our Story

Our Favorite Memories

Would We Recommend This To Others?   Yes ☐   No ☐
Would We Do It Again?   Yes ☐   No ☐

38

Date: _____

Why we want to do this.

_____
_____
_____
_____

Our Plan to make this happen.

_____
_____
_____
_____

⟵⟵⟵ ⟪⟪ **Let's Do This!** ⟫⟫ ⟶⟶⟶

Completion Date _____ **Location** _____

Our Story _____
_____
_____
_____
_____
_____

Our Favorite Memories
_____
_____
_____

Would We Recommend This To Others?   Yes ☐   No ☐
Would We Do It Again?   Yes ☐   No ☐

39

Date:

Why we want to do this.

Our Plan to make this happen.

←——————————⟪⟪ **Let's Do This!** ⟫⟫——————————→

Completion Date **Location**

Our Story

Our Favorite Memories

Would We Recommend This To Others?   Yes ☐   No ☐
Would We Do It Again?   Yes ☐   No ☐

40

Date: _____

_____
_____
_____

Why we want to do this.

_____
_____
_____
_____

Our Plan to make this happen.

_____
_____
_____
_____

⟵——————⟪⟪ **Let's Do This!** ⟫⟫——————⟶

Completion Date _____   **Location** _____

Our Story

_____
_____
_____
_____
_____
_____

Our Favorite Memories

_____
_____
_____

Would We Recommend This To Others?   Yes ☐   No ☐

Would We Do It Again?   Yes ☐   No ☐

41

Date:

Why we want to do this.

Our Plan to make this happen.

←——————————⋘ **Let's Do This!** ⋙——————————→

Completion Date　　　　　Location

Our Story

Our Favorite Memories

Would We Recommend This To Others?　Yes ☐　No ☐

Would We Do It Again?　Yes ☐　No ☐

42

Date: _____

Why we want to do this.

_____
_____
_____

Our Plan to make this happen.

_____
_____
_____

←——————— ⋘ Let's Do This! ⋙ ———————→

Completion Date _____   Location _____

Our Story

_____
_____
_____
_____

Our Favorite Memories

_____
_____
_____

Would We Recommend This To Others?   Yes ☐   No ☐
Would We Do It Again?   Yes ☐   No ☐

43

Date: _____

Why we want to do this.

Our Plan to make this happen.

⟵————— ⋘ Let's Do This! ⋙ —————⟶

Completion Date _____ **Location** _____

Our Story

Our Favorite Memories

Would We Recommend This To Others?   Yes ☐   No ☐
Would We Do It Again?   Yes ☐   No ☐

44

Date: _____

Why we want to do this.

Our Plan to make this happen.

⟵————— ⋘ **Let's Do This!** ⋙ —————⟶

Completion Date _____   **Location** _____

Our Story

Our Favorite Memories

Would We Recommend This To Others?   Yes ☐   No ☐
Would We Do It Again?   Yes ☐   No ☐

45

Date:

Why we want to do this.

Our Plan to make this happen.

<<< Let's Do This! >>>

Completion Date   Location

Our Story

Our Favorite Memories

Would We Recommend This To Others?   Yes ☐   No ☐
Would We Do It Again?   Yes ☐   No ☐

46

Date: _____

_____
_____

Why we want to do this.

_____
_____
_____
_____

Our Plan to make this happen.

_____
_____
_____
_____

⟵——————⟪⟪⟪ **Let's Do This!** ⟫⟫⟫——————⟶

Completion Date _____ **Location** _____

Our Story _____
_____
_____
_____
_____

Our Favorite Memories _____
_____
_____
_____

Would We Recommend This To Others?   Yes ☐   No ☐
Would We Do It Again?   Yes ☐   No ☐

47

Date:

Why we want to do this.

Our Plan to make this happen.

<<< Let's Do This! >>>

Completion Date   Location

Our Story

Our Favorite Memories

Would We Recommend This To Others?   Yes ☐   No ☐
Would We Do It Again?   Yes ☐   No ☐

48

Date: _____

Why we want to do this.
_____
_____
_____
_____

Our Plan to make this happen.
_____
_____
_____
_____

⟵————————⟪⟪⟪ Let's Do This! ⟫⟫⟫————————⟶

Completion Date _____   Location _____

Our Story
_____
_____
_____
_____
_____

Our Favorite Memories
_____
_____
_____

Would We Recommend This To Others?   Yes ☐   No ☐
Would We Do It Again?   Yes ☐   No ☐

49

Date: _____

Why we want to do this.

Our Plan to make this happen.

⟵————————⟪⟪⟪ **Let's Do This!** ⟫⟫⟫————————⟶

Completion Date _____   Location _____

Our Story

Our Favorite Memories

Would We Recommend This To Others?   Yes ☐   No ☐
Would We Do It Again?   Yes ☐   No ☐

50

Date: _____

Why we want to do this.

Our Plan to make this happen.

⟵ ⟪⟪⟪ **Let's Do This!** ⟫⟫⟫ ⟶

Completion Date _____ **Location** _____

Our Story

Our Favorite Memories

Would We Recommend This To Others?   Yes ☐   No ☐
Would We Do It Again?   Yes ☐   No ☐

51

Date:

Why we want to do this.

Our Plan to make this happen.

Let's Do This!

Completion Date   Location

Our Story

Our Favorite Memories

Would We Recommend This To Others?   Yes ☐   No ☐
Would We Do It Again?   Yes ☐   No ☐

52

Date: _____

_____
_____

Why we want to do this.
_____
_____
_____
_____

Our Plan to make this happen.
_____
_____
_____
_____

⟵————————⟪⟪⟪ **Let's Do This!** ⟫⟫⟫————————⟶

Completion Date _____ **Location** _____

Our Story
_____
_____
_____
_____
_____

Our Favorite Memories
_____
_____
_____

Would We Recommend This To Others? Yes ☐ No ☐
Would We Do It Again? Yes ☐ No ☐

53

Date: _____

Why we want to do this.

Our Plan to make this happen.

⟵ ⟪ Let's Do This! ⟫ ⟶

Completion Date _____ Location _____

Our Story

Our Favorite Memories

Would We Recommend This To Others?   Yes ☐   No ☐
Would We Do It Again?   Yes ☐   No ☐

54

Date: _____

Why we want to do this.

_____
_____
_____
_____

Our Plan to make this happen.

_____
_____
_____
_____

⟵ ⋘ **Let's Do This!** ⋙ ⟶

Completion Date _____ **Location** _____

Our Story

_____
_____
_____
_____
_____

Our Favorite Memories

_____
_____
_____

Would We Recommend This To Others?   Yes ☐   No ☐
Would We Do It Again?   Yes ☐   No ☐

55

Date: _____

Why we want to do this.

Our Plan to make this happen.

⟵———— ⟨⟨⟨ Let's Do This! ⟩⟩⟩ ————⟶

Completion Date _____   Location _____

Our Story

Our Favorite Memories

Would We Recommend This To Others?   Yes ☐   No ☐
Would We Do It Again?   Yes ☐   No ☐

56

Date: _____

Why we want to do this.

_____
_____
_____
_____

Our Plan to make this happen.

_____
_____
_____
_____

⟵ ⋘ **Let's Do This!** ⋙ ⟶

Completion Date _____ **Location** _____

Our Story

_____
_____
_____
_____
_____

Our Favorite Memories

_____
_____
_____

Would We Recommend This To Others?   Yes ☐   No ☐
Would We Do It Again?   Yes ☐   No ☐

57

Date:

Why we want to do this.

Our Plan to make this happen.

←——⟪⟪ Let's Do This! ⟫⟫——→

Completion Date   Location

Our Story

Our Favorite Memories

Would We Recommend This To Others?   Yes ☐   No ☐
Would We Do It Again?   Yes ☐   No ☐

58

Date: _____

_____
_____
_____

Why we want to do this.

_____
_____
_____
_____

Our Plan to make this happen.

_____
_____
_____
_____

⟵——————⟪⟪⟪ **Let's Do This!** ⟫⟫⟫——————⟶

Completion Date _____ **Location** _____

Our Story

_____
_____
_____
_____
_____

Our Favorite Memories

_____
_____
_____

Would We Recommend This To Others?   Yes ☐   No ☐
Would We Do It Again?   Yes ☐   No ☐

59

Date:

Why we want to do this.

Our Plan to make this happen.

⇐ ⋘ Let's Do This! ⋙ ⇒

Completion Date   Location

Our Story

Our Favorite Memories

Would We Recommend This To Others? Yes ☐ No ☐
Would We Do It Again? Yes ☐ No ☐

60

Date: _____

Why we want to do this.

Our Plan to make this happen.

⟵ ⟪ **Let's Do This!** ⟫ ⟶

Completion Date _____   **Location** _____

Our Story

Our Favorite Memories

Would We Recommend This To Others?   Yes ☐   No ☐
Would We Do It Again?   Yes ☐   No ☐

61

Date:

Why we want to do this.

Our Plan to make this happen.

⟵ ⟪ Let's Do This! ⟫ ⟶

Completion Date   Location

Our Story

Our Favorite Memories

Would We Recommend This To Others?   Yes ☐   No ☐
Would We Do It Again?   Yes ☐   No ☐

62

Date: _____

Why we want to do this.

_____
_____
_____
_____

Our Plan to make this happen.

_____
_____
_____
_____

⟵ ⟪⟪⟪ **Let's Do This!** ⟫⟫⟫ ⟶

Completion Date _____ **Location** _____

Our Story _____

_____
_____
_____
_____
_____

Our Favorite Memories

_____
_____
_____
_____

Would We Recommend This To Others? Yes ☐   No ☐
Would We Do It Again? Yes ☐   No ☐

63

Date: _____

Why we want to do this.

_____
_____
_____
_____

Our Plan to make this happen.

_____
_____
_____
_____

⟵——————⋘ **Let's Do This!** ⋙——————⟶

Completion Date _____ Location _____

Our Story

_____
_____
_____
_____
_____
_____

Our Favorite Memories

_____
_____
_____

Would We Recommend This To Others?   Yes ☐   No ☐
Would We Do It Again?   Yes ☐   No ☐

64

Date: _____

_____
_____

Why we want to do this.

_____
_____
_____
_____

Our Plan to make this happen.

_____
_____
_____
_____

⟵────── ⟪⟪ **Let's Do This!** ⟫⟫ ──────⟶

Completion Date _____   **Location** _____

Our Story _____

_____
_____
_____
_____

Our Favorite Memories

_____
_____
_____

Would We Recommend This To Others?   Yes ☐   No ☐
Would We Do It Again?   Yes ☐   No ☐

65

Date: _____

Why we want to do this.

Our Plan to make this happen.

⟵——————— ⋘ Let's Do This! ⋙ ———————⟶

Completion Date   Location

Our Story

Our Favorite Memories

Would We Recommend This To Others?   Yes ☐   No ☐

Would We Do It Again?   Yes ☐   No ☐

66

Date: _____

_____

_____

Why we want to do this.

_____
_____
_____
_____

Our Plan to make this happen.

_____
_____
_____
_____

←——————— ⋘ **Let's Do This!** ⋙ ———————→

Completion Date _____   **Location** _____

Our Story

_____
_____
_____
_____
_____
_____

Our Favorite Memories

_____
_____
_____

Would We Recommend This To Others?   Yes ☐   No ☐
Would We Do It Again?   Yes ☐   No ☐

67

Date: _____

Why we want to do this.

Our Plan to make this happen.

←←← **Let's Do This!** →→→

Completion Date _____ **Location** _____

Our Story

Our Favorite Memories

Would We Recommend This To Others?   Yes ☐   No ☐
Would We Do It Again?   Yes ☐   No ☐

68

Date: _____

Why we want to do this.

Our Plan to make this happen.

<<< **Let's Do This!** >>>

Completion Date _____ **Location** _____

Our Story

Our Favorite Memories

Would We Recommend This To Others?   Yes ☐   No ☐
Would We Do It Again?   Yes ☐   No ☐

69

Date:

Why we want to do this.

Our Plan to make this happen.

Let's Do This!

Completion Date _____ Location _____

Our Story

Our Favorite Memories

Would We Recommend This To Others? Yes ☐ No ☐
Would We Do It Again? Yes ☐ No ☐

70

Date: _____

_____
_____

Why we want to do this.

_____
_____
_____
_____

Our Plan to make this happen.

_____
_____
_____
_____

⟵——————— ⟪ **Let's Do This!** ⟫ ———————⟶

Completion Date _____   **Location** _____

Our Story

_____
_____
_____
_____
_____

Our Favorite Memories

_____
_____
_____

Would We Recommend This To Others?   Yes ☐   No ☐
Would We Do It Again?   Yes ☐   No ☐

71

Date:

Why we want to do this.

Our Plan to make this happen.

⟵──────────⟪ Let's Do This! ⟫──────────⟶

Completion Date   Location

Our Story

Our Favorite Memories

Would We Recommend This To Others?   Yes ☐   No ☐

Would We Do It Again?   Yes ☐   No ☐

72

Date: _____

Why we want to do this.

Our Plan to make this happen.

⟵——————⟪⟪⟪ Let's Do This! ⟫⟫⟫——————⟶

Completion Date _____ Location _____

Our Story

Our Favorite Memories

Would We Recommend This To Others? Yes ☐   No ☐
Would We Do It Again?   Yes ☐   No ☐

73

Date:

Why we want to do this.

Our Plan to make this happen.

<<< Let's Do This! >>>

Completion Date   Location

Our Story

Our Favorite Memories

Would We Recommend This To Others?   Yes ☐   No ☐
Would We Do It Again?   Yes ☐   No ☐

74

Date: _____

Why we want to do this.

Our Plan to make this happen.

⟵———————⋘ Let's Do This! ⋙———————⟶

Completion Date _____ **Location** _____

Our Story

Our Favorite Memories

Would We Recommend This To Others? Yes ☐ No ☐
Would We Do It Again? Yes ☐ No ☐

75

Date: _____

Why we want to do this.

Our Plan to make this happen.

⟵⟵⟵ Let's Do This! ⟶⟶⟶

Completion Date _____ Location _____

Our Story

Our Favorite Memories

Would We Recommend This To Others? Yes ☐ No ☐

Would We Do It Again? Yes ☐ No ☐

76

Date: _____

_____

_____

Why we want to do this.

_____
_____
_____
_____

Our Plan to make this happen.

_____
_____
_____
_____

⟵——————⟪⟪⟪ **Let's Do This!** ⟫⟫⟫——————⟶

Completion Date _____   **Location** _____

Our Story

_____
_____
_____
_____
_____
_____

Our Favorite Memories

_____
_____
_____

Would We Recommend This To Others?   Yes ☐   No ☐

Would We Do It Again?   Yes ☐   No ☐

77

Date:

Why we want to do this.

Our Plan to make this happen.

⟵ ⟪ Let's Do This! ⟫ ⟶

Completion Date   Location

Our Story

Our Favorite Memories

Would We Recommend This To Others?   Yes ☐   No ☐
Would We Do It Again?   Yes ☐   No ☐

78

Date: _____

Why we want to do this.

_____
_____
_____
_____

Our Plan to make this happen.

_____
_____
_____
_____

⟵————————⟪⟪⟪ **Let's Do This!** ⟫⟫⟫————————⟶

Completion Date _____ **Location** _____

Our Story _____
_____
_____
_____
_____
_____

Our Favorite Memories _____
_____
_____
_____

Would We Recommend This To Others? Yes ☐   No ☐

Would We Do It Again?   Yes ☐   No ☐

79

Date:

Why we want to do this.

Our Plan to make this happen.

Let's Do This!

Completion Date   Location

Our Story

Our Favorite Memories

Would We Recommend This To Others?   Yes ☐   No ☐
Would We Do It Again?   Yes ☐   No ☐

80

Date:

Why we want to do this.

Our Plan to make this happen.

Let's Do This!

Completion Date   Location

Our Story

Our Favorite Memories

Would We Recommend This To Others?   Yes ☐   No ☐
Would We Do It Again?   Yes ☐   No ☐

81

Date:

Why we want to do this.

Our Plan to make this happen.

←——————⟪⟪ Let's Do This! ⟫⟫——————→

Completion Date   Location

Our Story

Our Favorite Memories

Would We Recommend This To Others?   Yes ☐   No ☐
Would We Do It Again?   Yes ☐   No ☐

82

Date: _____

_____
_____

Why we want to do this.

_____
_____
_____
_____

Our Plan to make this happen.

_____
_____
_____
_____

⟵——————⟪⟪ **Let's Do This!** ⟫⟫——————⟶

Completion Date _____   **Location** _____

Our Story

_____
_____
_____
_____
_____

Our Favorite Memories

_____
_____
_____

Would We Recommend This To Others?   Yes ☐   No ☐
Would We Do It Again?   Yes ☐   No ☐

83

Date:

Why we want to do this.

Our Plan to make this happen.

Let's Do This!

Completion Date   Location

Our Story

Our Favorite Memories

Would We Recommend This To Others?   Yes ☐   No ☐
Would We Do It Again?   Yes ☐   No ☐

84

Date: _____

Why we want to do this.

_____
_____
_____

Our Plan to make this happen.

_____
_____
_____

←――――――― ⋘ **Let's Do This!** ⋙ ―――――――→

Completion Date _____ **Location** _____

Our Story

_____
_____
_____
_____

Our Favorite Memories

_____
_____
_____

Would We Recommend This To Others?   Yes ☐   No ☐
Would We Do It Again?   Yes ☐   No ☐

85

Date: _____

Why we want to do this.

_____
_____
_____

Our Plan to make this happen.

_____
_____
_____

⟵————————⟨⟨⟨ Let's Do This! ⟩⟩⟩————————⟶

Completion Date _____   Location _____

Our Story

_____
_____
_____
_____

Our Favorite Memories

_____
_____

Would We Recommend This To Others?   Yes ☐   No ☐
Would We Do It Again?   Yes ☐   No ☐

Copyrighted Material

86

Date: _____

Why we want to do this.

_____
_____
_____

Our Plan to make this happen.

_____
_____
_____

⟵ ⋘ **Let's Do This!** ⋙ ⟶

Completion Date _____ **Location** _____

Our Story

_____
_____
_____
_____
_____

Our Favorite Memories

_____
_____
_____

Would We Recommend This To Others? Yes ☐ No ☐
Would We Do It Again? Yes ☐ No ☐

87

Date:

Why we want to do this.

Our Plan to make this happen.

⟵————— ⋘ Let's Do This! ⋙ —————⟶

Completion Date   Location

Our Story

Our Favorite Memories

Would We Recommend This To Others?   Yes ☐   No ☐
Would We Do It Again?   Yes ☐   No ☐

88

Date:

Why we want to do this.

Our Plan to make this happen.

Let's Do This!

Completion Date   **Location**

Our Story

Our Favorite Memories

Would We Recommend This To Others?   Yes ☐   No ☐
Would We Do It Again?   Yes ☐   No ☐

89

Date:

Why we want to do this.

Our Plan to make this happen.

⟵ ⋘ Let's Do This! ⋙ ⟶

Completion Date   Location

Our Story

Our Favorite Memories

Would We Recommend This To Others?   Yes ☐   No ☐
Would We Do It Again?   Yes ☐   No ☐

90

Date: _____

Why we want to do this.

Our Plan to make this happen.

⟵―――――⟪ Let's Do This! ⟫―――――⟶

Completion Date _____ **Location** _____

Our Story

Our Favorite Memories

Would We Recommend This To Others?   Yes ☐   No ☐
Would We Do It Again?   Yes ☐   No ☐

91

Date:

Why we want to do this.

Our Plan to make this happen.

⟵——— ⋘ **Let's Do This!** ⋙ ———⟶

Completion Date　　　　**Location**

Our Story

Our Favorite Memories

Would We Recommend This To Others?　Yes ☐　No ☐
Would We Do It Again?　Yes ☐　No ☐

92

Date: _____

Why we want to do this.

_____
_____
_____

Our Plan to make this happen.

_____
_____
_____

⟵⟪ Let's Do This! ⟫⟶

Completion Date _____ **Location** _____

Our Story

_____
_____
_____
_____

Our Favorite Memories

_____
_____

Would We Recommend This To Others?   Yes ☐   No ☐
Would We Do It Again?   Yes ☐   No ☐

93

Date: _____

Why we want to do this.

Our Plan to make this happen.

⟵————————— ⋘ **Let's Do This!** ⋙ —————————⟶

Completion Date _____ Location _____

Our Story

Our Favorite Memories

Would We Recommend This To Others?   Yes ☐   No ☐

Would We Do It Again?   Yes ☐   No ☐

94

Date: _____

Why we want to do this.

Our Plan to make this happen.

←——————— ⋘ **Let's Do This!** ⋙ ———————→

Completion Date _____   Location _____

Our Story

Our Favorite Memories

Would We Recommend This To Others?   Yes ☐   No ☐
Would We Do It Again?   Yes ☐   No ☐

95

Date:

Why we want to do this.

Our Plan to make this happen.

⟵——————— ⋘ Let's Do This! ⋙ ———————⟶

Completion Date   Location

Our Story

Our Favorite Memories

Would We Recommend This To Others?   Yes ☐   No ☐
Would We Do It Again?   Yes ☐   No ☐

96

Date:

Why we want to do this.

Our Plan to make this happen.

Let's Do This!

Completion Date   Location

Our Story

Our Favorite Memories

Would We Recommend This To Others?   Yes ☐   No ☐
Would We Do It Again?   Yes ☐   No ☐

97

Date:

Why we want to do this.

Our Plan to make this happen.

<<< **Let's Do This!** >>>

Completion Date   **Location**

Our Story

Our Favorite Memories

Would We Recommend This To Others?   Yes ☐   No ☐
Would We Do It Again?   Yes ☐   No ☐

98

Date: _____

Why we want to do this.

Our Plan to make this happen.

⟵ ⟪⟪ Let's Do This! ⟫⟫ ⟶

Completion Date _____   Location _____

Our Story

Our Favorite Memories

Would We Recommend This To Others?   Yes ☐   No ☐
Would We Do It Again?   Yes ☐   No ☐

99

Date:

Why we want to do this.

Our Plan to make this happen.

⟵―――――⋘ Let's Do This! ⋙―――――⟶

Completion Date   Location

Our Story

Our Favorite Memories

Would We Recommend This To Others?   Yes ☐   No ☐
Would We Do It Again?   Yes ☐   No ☐

100

Date:

Why we want to do this.

Our Plan to make this happen.

<<< **Let's Do This!** >>>

Completion Date **Location**

Our Story

Our Favorite Memories

Would We Recommend This To Others?   Yes ☐   No ☐
Would We Do It Again?   Yes ☐   No ☐

Printed in Great Britain
by Amazon